CAN YOU HELP PHOENIX FIND THESE ITEMS IN THE BOOK?

CAPTAIN SEA WHISKERS TOY 1

CAPTAIN SEA WHISKERS BOOK 2

SOCCER BALL 2

CALENDAR 1

PET CAT 3

PAIR OF BOOTS 1

MAGNIFYING GLASS 2

BADGE 3

Helper

PhoenixSoulWarrior.com

Text copyright © 2021 by Heather Yaskiw Foisy
Illustrations copyright © 2021 by Daniel Naranjo
Published by Foisy Fur Friends ®

Library of Congress Cataloging-in-Publication Data

Name: Foisy, Heather, author. Daniel Naranjo, illustrator.
Title: I'm the Biggest Helper With Momma's Autoimmune Disease / Heather Foisy; illustrated by Daniel Naranjo
Summary: A child teaches the reader about autoimmune diseases and how they work in the body. The child goes on to describe the many ways he helps his mother who has multiple autoimmune diseases (Sjögren's and lupus).
Subjects: Children – Fiction, People with disabilities – Fiction, Helping – Fiction
Identifiers:
ISBN (Hardcopy book): 978-1-7776810-0-5
ISBN (ebook): 978-1-7776810-1-2

Words by Heather Yaskiw Foisy ● Edits by Raina Schnider ● Illustrations by Daniel Naranjo
Created in Canada ● Illustrated in Colombia ● Published in Canada ● Printed in China

First Edition, 2021
10 9 8 7 6 5 4 3 2 1

This book can be purchased in bulk for promotional, educational and business use.
Contact your local bookseller or contact Foisy Fur Friends at PhoenixSoulWarrior@gmail.com

To Phoenix,

Thank you for becoming my biggest helper.

Your courage and compassion are the inspiration for this book.

Today I want to share
About all the things I do
To be the biggest helper
So you can be one too!

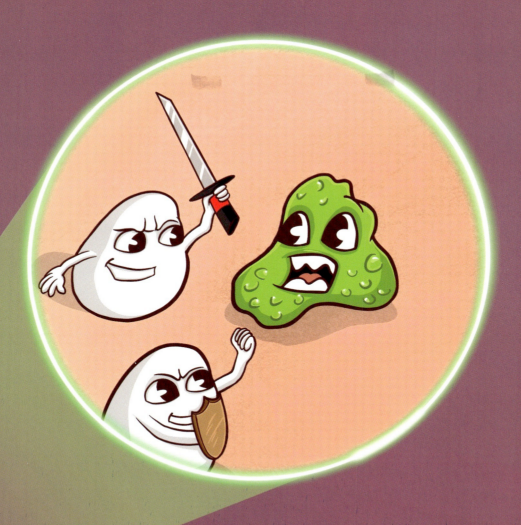

My momma has this illness
Called an autoimmune disease,
But you would never know it
Because it's an illness you can't see.

Everyone has an immune system
Designed to fight invaders.
So when bacteria and viruses attack
The immune system kills those raiders.

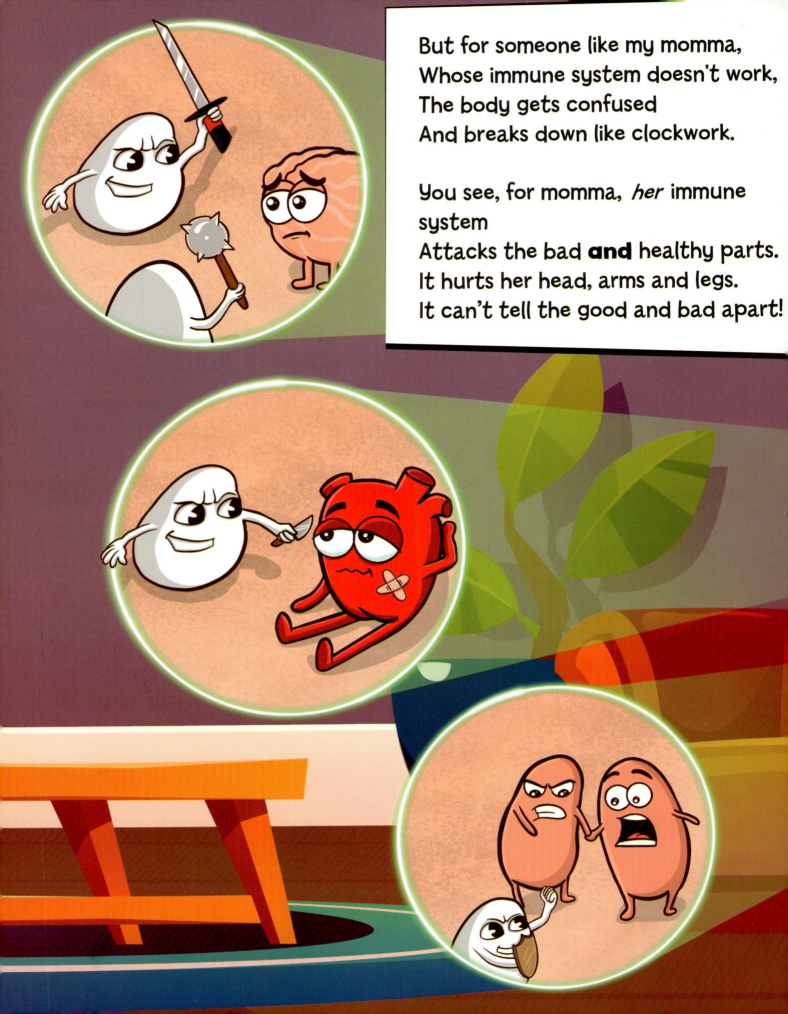

But for someone like my momma,
Whose immune system doesn't work,
The body gets confused
And breaks down like clockwork.

You see, for momma, *her* immune system
Attacks the bad **and** healthy parts.
It hurts her head, arms and legs.
It can't tell the good and bad apart!

This means my momma hurts sometimes
On the inside without a sight.
The same way you or I might hurt
from a cut, bruise, or bite.

My momma has more than one illness,
As people often do.
Sjögren's [show-grins] is its name.
Another one is lupus [loo-pus] too.

Lots of people around the world
Need help with these illnesses.
There are lots of different kinds
And their names can sound like this:

Multiple sclerosis [skli-roh-sis]
Is one my grandma has.
Type 1 diabetes
Like my uncle and my aunts.

Crohn's [krohnz] disease, celiac [se-le-ak] disease
And rheumatoid [roo-muh-toid] arthritis [ahr-thrahy-tis].
A few more that I know about are
Psoriasis [suh-rahy-uh-sis] and vasculitis [vas-kyuh-lahy-tis].

Every type of autoimmune disease
Can hurt in a different way.
We can't always see the pain,
So we should be kind every day.

That's why the world needs helpers
Just like you and me
To aid them with their troubles
So we can help them feel happy!

I'm the biggest helper
And there's lots that I can do
To help my momma when she's sick
So she doesn't feel so blue.

At times I push the cart.
I also help pick out the food.
And if my momma can't walk that day
I push the wheelchair too!

I'm fond of helping with the chores,
Like raking up the leaves
Or shoveling snow off the sidewalk
To help my momma's knees.

When momma's arms are hurting
And the plants need to be fed,
I unravel the hose and move it
Then I water the flower bed.

When momma cooks our supper
Yummy pasta and buttered roll
I help to set the table
With forks, knives and bowls.

I bring the dishes to the sink
After we eat dessert.
I wash the dishes to get them clean.
I scrub off all the dirt.

Playing is a lot of fun
And the house gets quite untidy.
My toys get scattered across the room,
So I clean up every Friday.

I try to keep my room spotless.
I look from wall to wall.
Then I pick up my own toys,
So momma doesn't trip and fall.

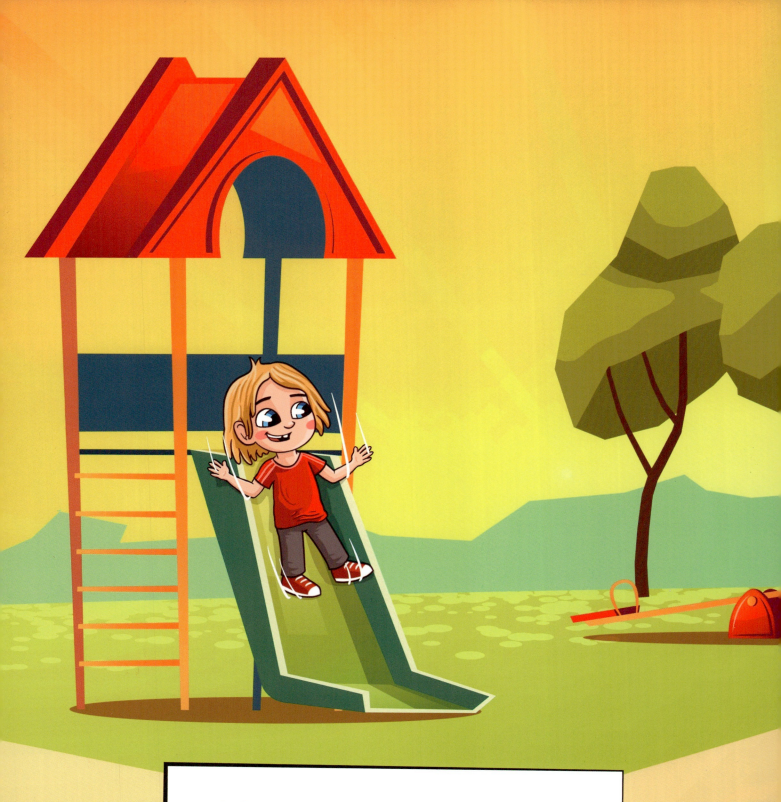

I always ask my momma
On days she's feeling great
If we can go outside and play
And on those days, we stay up late.

On days that we go to the park
The swing is my go-to ride,
But if her arms hurt too much
I jump over to the slide.

On days that momma hurts too much,
If she just can't move a bit,
I will read and sing and colour
Around her while she sits.

On those same days that momma hurts,
If she can't get out of bed,
I give her cuddles and kisses
While laying down instead.

Now that I am done sharing
About all the things I do
To be the biggest helper
Now you can be one too!

Glossary, References & Notes:

Glossary

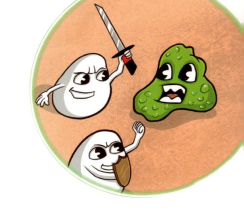

The **immune system** is a complex organization inside the body that is designed to seek and destroy invaders of the body, including bacteria, viruses and other foreign attackers.

An **autoimmune disease** is an illness that causes the immune system to attack itself. This means that the immune system does not distinguish between healthy tissues and harmful attackers like bacteria and viruses. As a result, the body sets off a reaction that destroys normal tissues.

Sjögren's, pronounced "show-grins," is an autoimmune disease in which the body attacks primarily moisture-producing glands such as the mouth and eyes. Sjögren's is systemic, meaning it can attack the entire body. Joint pain and fatigue are the most common symptoms; however, this disease can attack and destroy any organ in the body.

Lupus is a systemic autoimmune disease. There are four different kinds of lupus, but Systemic Lupus Erythematosus (SLE) is the most common. SLE primarily attacks the joints, skin, kidneys, blood cells, brain, heart and lungs. SLE is related to Sjögren's; both diseases have overlap in symptoms, and are sometimes called sister diseases.

Multiple sclerosis is a chronic, typically progressive autoimmune disease involving damage to the nerve cells in the brain and spinal cord. Symptoms of this disease typically involve numbness, impairment of speech, impairment of muscular coordination, blurred vision and severe fatigue.

Crohn's disease is a chronic autoimmune disease that causes inflammation and irritation to the digestive tract. Symptoms often include abdominal pain, diarrhea and weight loss.

Celiac disease is an autoimmune disease that is triggered when a person eats gluten. Gluten is a protein found in wheat, rye, barley and other grains. When a person with celiac disease eats gluten, their body reacts to the protein causing damage to the small intestine.

Rheumatoid arthritis is a chronic progressive autoimmune disease that causes inflammation in the joints. This disease can cause painful deformity of the joints and immobility of the joints. The joints often impacted are the fingers, wrists, feet and ankles.

Psoriasis is a chronic autoimmune condition of the skin where the skin cells multiply ten times faster than normal. This causes skin to build up resulting in bumpy red patches and white scales.

Vasculitis is an autoimmune disease that results in inflammation of your blood cells. This causes thickening, weakening, narrowing, or scarring of the blood vessel walls. These changes can restrict blood flow, resulting in organ and tissue damage.

References:

There are over 100 autoimmune diseases as reported by American Autoimmune Related Diseases Association (aarda.org).

Notes:

The inspiration for this book was the author's son, who at the age of 4 became her biggest helper. The stories shared in this book reflect the various ways he helped her manage day-to-day life with debilitating symptoms caused by her autoimmune disease.

You may be wondering how the author chose the autoimmune diseases listed in the book, considering there are over 100 different kinds.

The author has been diagnosed with Sjögren's and lupus, in addition to being monitored for vasculitis. The additional autoimmune conditions listed in the book are conditions of close family members including her maternal grandfather, mother, sister and brother.

Did you like this book? Are you wondering how you can help?

This book was self-published, which means from conception to hard copy, our family did all the leg work.

There are many ways that you can help a book author like myself. My first suggestion is to share this book with your friends and family. Bring it to your next family gathering, have your child share it at school, or order the book as a gift for a special family member.

With your support we can get this book into the hands of many families, all over the globe.

I believe this story can help change the world and make it a better place. If you believe this too, please consider sharing this book.

Thank you, from the bottom of my heart, for all your support.

About the Author

Heather was diagnosed with Sjögren's, a systemic autoimmune disease, at the age of 28. She continued to live a relatively normal life and did so successfully by getting married, having a child, building a successful career and traveling the world.

In 2017, her health went haywire. Sadly her Sjögren's went into a regression (also called a flare up) and at that time she was also diagnosed with lupus.

Since then Heather has reduced her work hours to spend time healing. Heather enjoys giving back to the autoimmune disease and chronic illness communities. She has done so by volunteering as the Calgary Support Group Leader for the Sjögren's Society of Canada, starting a website and blog (PhoenixSoulWarrior.com) dedicated to educating and empowering Sjögren's and lupus patients, and writing this book to help describe how wonderful it is to have a helper like her young son.

Heather lives in Calgary, Alberta, Canada with her husband Marc, her son Phoenix and her three cats. She enjoys spending time in nature and runs away to spend time in the Rocky Mountains as often as she can and when her body allows.